From the Editors of OWL Magazine

© 2008 Bayard Canada Books, Inc.

Publisher: Jennifer Canham
Associate Publisher: Angela Keenlyside
Editorial Director: Mary Beth Leatherdale
Creative Director: Barb Kelly
Editors: Katherine Dearlove, John Crossingham
Production Coordinator: Paul Markowski
Production Editor: Larissa Byj
Production Assistant: Kathy Ko

Designer: Kathe Gray Design
Cover Illustration: Aaron Leighton

We gratefully acknowledge the financial support of the Government of Canada through the Book Publishing Industry Development Program (BPIDP) for our publishing activities.

Canada Council   Conseil des Arts
for the Arts   du Canada

Library and Archives Canada Cataloguing in Publication
Try this at home : planet-friendly projects for kids / Jackie Farquhar, D.I.Y. editor.

ISBN 978-2-89579-192-8

1. Environmental education – Activity programs – Juvenile literature.
2. Environmental protection – Juvenile literature. I. Farquhar, Jackie, 1975-

GE115.T79 2008   j333.72   C2007-907460-X

FSC Mixed Sources
Product group from well-managed forests, controlled sources and recycled wood or fibre
www.fsc.org Cert no. SW-COC-1271
© 1996 Forest Stewardship Council

Printed and bound in Canada

Owlkids Publishing
10 Lower Spadina Ave., Suite 400
Toronto, ON M5V 2Z2
Ph: 416-340-2700
Fax: 416-340-9769

Publisher of

chirp chickaDEE OWL

www.owlkids.com

BLT 3/29/11

TRY this at HOME

Planet-friendly Projects for Kids

Owl kids

Contents

Hi, I'm Jackie.
I'm the D.I.Y. — that's "Do It Yourself" — editor for OWL.
I try all the crafts and activities that go in the magazine.

Did you know that eating pizza can be good for the environment?
What about punking out your wardrobe? We put this book
together to let you in on some of the planet-friendly fun stuff
we've talked about in OWL. You'll also find out some important
info about our world — and how to keep it clean, green, and
healthy — along the way.

Hope you enjoy the book as much as we do!

Jackie

Jackie Farquhar
D.I.Y. Editor

The next time
You want to buy something
something

BUY VINTAGE FASHIONS AT SECOND-HAND STORES.

LOOK FOR CERTIFIED ORGANIC CLOTHING. IT'S MADE FROM FABRICS FREE OF HERBICIDES OR PESTICIDES.

WHAT YOU'LL NEED

➤ T-shirt (a light-coloured one will work best)
➤ computer
➤ printer
➤ T-shirt transfer paper for your printer
➤ scissors
➤ iron
➤ ironing board

Wear It's At

Got some old threads that could use a makeover? Take your favourite phrase and turn that dull shirt into a go-to tee!

1 Choose a word or saying to put on your shirt. Type it into a word-processing document using a cool font.

IMPORTANT: Before you print, reverse the words so they'll be backwards when you print them.

2 Print your word or saying onto the transfer paper and trim the paper around the words.

3 Place your T-shirt on an ironing board. Lay the transfer paper, printed side down, exactly where you want the words to go. Iron the transfer for about 10 to 15 seconds per section until you've ironed the entire sheet.

4 Let the transfer sheet cool for about a minute before you touch it. Then slowly peel off the paper.

5 Show off your new threads to all your friends!

WHAT YOU'LL NEED

- T-shirt
- ribbon
- scissors
- ruler

All Tied Up

Use ribbon to add some style to an old tee.

2.5 cm (1 in.)

1 Make two rows of small cuts along one side of your T-shirt, from under the sleeves to the hem.
- The cuts should be as wide as the ribbon you're using.
- The cuts in each row should be about 2.5 cm (1 in.) apart.

2 Starting from the bottom, thread the ribbon through the cuts, up one row and down the other.

3 Scrunch up the shirt and tie the ribbon at the bottom.

4 Repeat on the other side of the shirt.

14

WHAT YOU'LL NEED

➤ T-shirt
➤ thick paper
➤ scissors
➤ fabric paint
➤ paint brush

USE A STENCIL TO
SHAKE UP A TEE
PROJECT
3

Paint by Numbers

Add some personality to your school clothes with a few quick brushstrokes.

1 Pick a number and draw it on a piece of thick paper. Carefully cut out the number to make a stencil.

2 Place the stencil on the front of the T-shirt and paint over it. Let it dry overnight.

15

TURN AN OLD SHIRT · INTO A NEW SHIRT

PROJECT 4

- T-shirt
- old T-shirts with interesting patches or decals
- scissors
- needle and thread

Get Sporty

Keep wearing your favourite sports shirts, even after you've outgrown them.

1 Cut off your favourite parts from your old sports shirts.

2 Hand-stitch the old parts onto a colourful plain T-shirt.

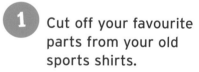

WHAT YOU'LL NEED

- a tank top or T-shirt
- sequin trim
- scissors
- needle and thread

Add It On

Give an old top a facelift. Stitch on some trim and you'll have a cool new design.

1 Choose strips of sequin trim that look great with an old tank top or T-shirt.

2 Stitch the trim to the shirt using a needle and thread.

Did you know?

Some charities make brand-new items by recycling the best parts of used clothing. So rather than throwing out your worn-outs, give your duds a new home.

➤ patch
➤ wool hat
➤ fabric glue

Use Your Head

Revive your interest in a well-worn hat. Glue a fabric patch to the front of a cap. Just make sure it's dry before you wear it out in the cold!

patch   **fabric glue**   **wool hat**

TIP: You could also try this with hats made of other materials, but a knitted hat works especially well because of the way the glue sticks to the wool fibres.

WHAT YOU'LL NEED

- apple
- pear
- knife
- canvas bag
- acrylic paint

PERSONALIZE
PROJECT
7
A CANVAS BAG

Bag It

Watch a bag go from drab to fab in a few easy steps. Cut some fruit in half, brush with paint, then stamp the painted side onto the bag.

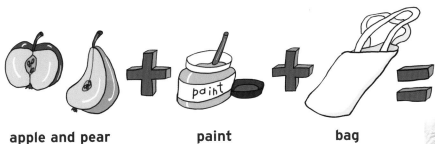

apple and pear   paint   bag

Did you know?

Every year, millions of plastic bags are made, used once, and then thrown away. Help make plastic bags history by asking stores to use biodegradable bags made from cornstarch instead. Better yet, bring your own canvas shopping bags. Your family may never use plastic again!

WHAT YOU'LL NEED

➤ thick elastic
➤ nuts of different sizes
➤ washers
➤ springs
➤ scissors

Hard Wear

There are more than just tools in a tool box. You can also find yourself the nuts and bolts of a rockin' new bracelet.

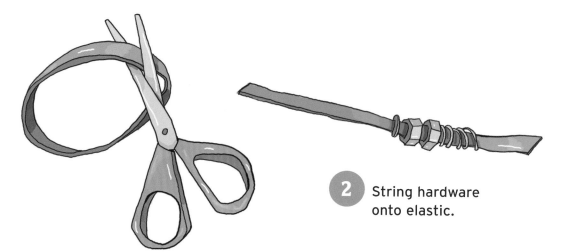

1 Cut elastic so it's one long piece.

2 String hardware onto elastic.

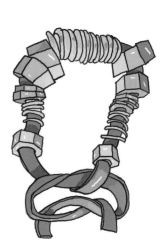

3 Knot ends of elastic together firmly. Trim extra elastic.

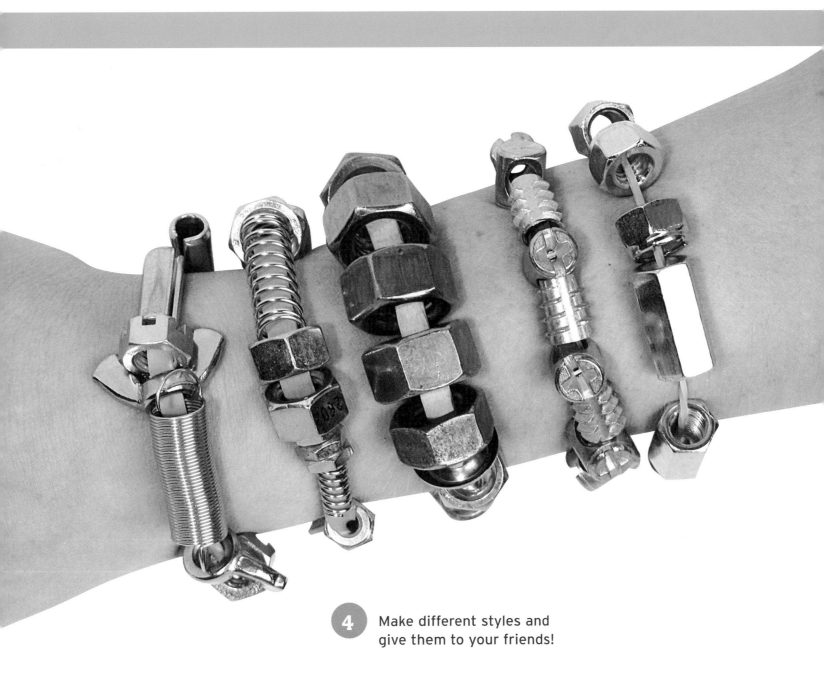

4 Make different styles and give them to your friends!

WHAT YOU'LL NEED

➤ old pair of socks
➤ scissors

➤ needle and thread
   (optional)

Sock 'Em

Cut the feet off an old pair of socks to make these stylish wrist warmers.

Cut the sock just above the ankle.

TIP: Fold the frayed edges under and sew for a neater look.

- ➤ old belt with a clasping belt buckle
- ➤ two rolls of duct tape (two different colours)
- ➤ scissors

Belt It Out

With an old belt and a couple of rolls of duct tape, you can keep your pants on in style.

1 Cover the belt in one colour of duct tape.

2 Cut out squares about 2.5 cm x 2.5 cm (1 in. x 1 in.) of the other colour.

3 Stick the squares on top, in a checkerboard pattern, wrapping the excess tape around the edge of the belt.

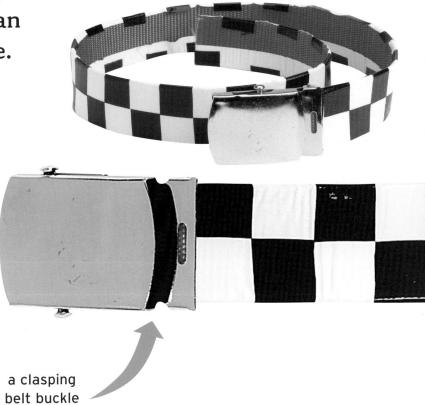

a clasping belt buckle

23

INSTEAD OF BUYING GIFTS,
TURN YOUR OLD STUFF INTO
SOMETHING NEW.

HANDMADE GIFTS ARE <u>BEST</u>
BECAUSE THEY'RE ONE OF A KIND
AND COME FROM THE ♥.

PROJECT **11**

WHAT YOU'LL NEED

- large shoebox
- paper
- 2 small plastic fruit baskets
- 8 long skewers
- 8 corks
- 6 clothespins
- small light ball
- paint
- tape
- scissors
- ruler
- markers

Funky Foosball

Want hours of entertainment for you and your friends? All you need is a bit of time and a few supplies.

1 Paint the inside of the shoebox to look like a soccer field. Write the stadium name on a piece of paper and tape it on the outside.

2 Cut a rectangular hole on each end of the shoebox and tape fruit baskets over the holes to make two goal boxes.

3 Poke four holes on each side of the box. Use a ruler to make sure they are evenly spaced.

4 Tape the skewers together so they overlap in the middle to make four extra-long skewers.

5 Stick the skewers through the holes and put a cork on each end. Attach the clothespins to the skewers.

6 Throw in the ball and…

"Game On!"

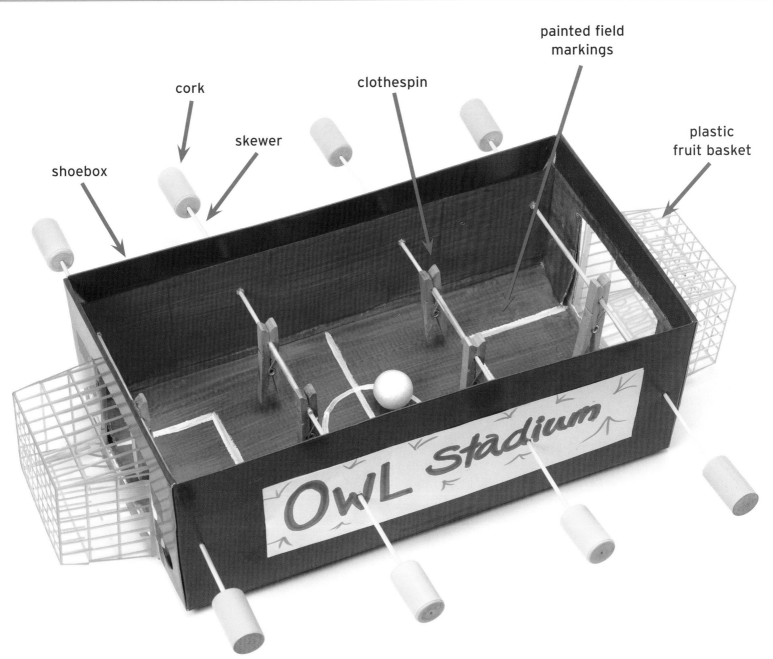

cork

skewer

clothespin

painted field markings

plastic fruit basket

shoebox

OwL Stadium

WHAT YOU'LL NEED

- ➤ 2 pieces of fabric larger than your gadget (felt and denim work well)
- ➤ fabric glue

- ➤ 5 cm (2 in.) of Velcro tape
- ➤ needle and yarn (optional)

- ➤ decorations such as beads, buttons, fabric paint, fabric flowers

Crafty Cozy

This gadget cozy will keep your MP3 player or cellphone clean and scratch-free.

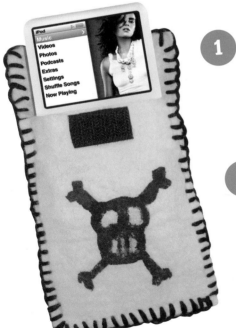

1 Cut one piece of fabric so it's 4 cm (1.5 in.) wider than the gadget. Make the second piece longer at the top for the flap.

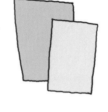

2 Glue along three edges. Leave the top edge open.

3 Glue Velcro on the inside of the top flap and on the front of the pocket.

4 Decorate your cozy with fabric paint, buttons, or plastic flowers.

5 For added strength, sew the edges with your choice of stitch.

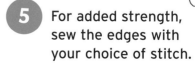

- empty CD case
  (thick ones work best)
- photo
- decorations such as
  candy, Popsicle sticks,
  stickers, paint, etc.
- glue
- tape

MAKE OLD CD CASES
PROJECT
13
PICTURE-PERFECT

Framed

Transform old CD cases into personalized picture frames.

1. Decorate the front cover of a CD case. Use candy, stickers, paint, plastic flowers – whatever you like! Let dry for one hour.

2. Cut a photo to fit in the front cover and tape to the inside. Open the CD case and stand upright to display.

WHAT YOU'LL NEED

- 45 mL (3 tbsp.) oatmeal
- 1 large bar of soap (try Ivory or Dove)
- 45 mL (3 tbsp.) water
- food colouring
- microwaveable bowl
- cheese grater
- cookie cutters
- baking tray

Stylish Suds

Good clean fun for everyone! These colourful hand soaps are great for your skin. Make some for your friends, but be sure to keep a few for yourself, too.

1 Break up the oatmeal flakes with your hands.

2 Grate the soap into small slivers using a cheese grater.

3 Place the soap slivers and the water in a large, microwaveable bowl.

4 Microwave on high for about 40 seconds, or until the soap bubbles are close to the bowl's edge. Stir and repeat until all slivers have melted.

REMEMBER: Get an adult's permission before using the microwave.

5 Mix in the oatmeal and two or three drops of food colouring. Spoon the mixture into cookie cutters placed on a flat tray.

6 Put the tray in the freezer for about an hour. Once they've cooled, pop out the soaps.

7 Store in a dry place. Use the ideas on the next page to wrap up your cool gifts.

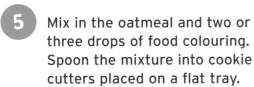

Did you know?

You can make a chemical-free face-cleansing mask by mixing 10 mL (2 tsp.) of plain yogurt, 5 mL (1 tsp.) of honey, and 5 mL (1 tsp.) of oatmeal. Gently rub the mixture onto your face. Let the mask dry for 15 minutes, then remove with a warm, damp cloth.

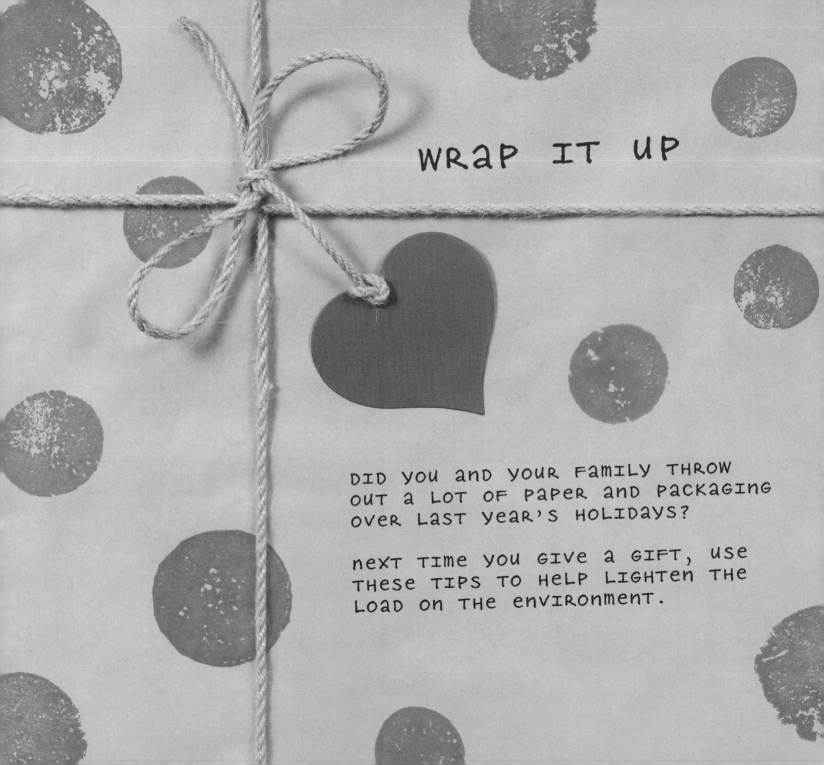

WRAP IT UP

DID YOU AND YOUR FAMILY THROW OUT A LOT OF PAPER AND PACKAGING OVER LAST YEAR'S HOLIDAYS?

NEXT TIME YOU GIVE A GIFT, USE THESE TIPS TO HELP LIGHTEN THE LOAD ON THE ENVIRONMENT.

SKIP THE WRAP! HIDE GIFTS AROUND THE HOUSE AND THEN HAVE A TREASURE HUNT.

ASK FOR GIFTS WITH LESS PACKAGING.

USE STUFF FROM AROUND THE HOUSE TO MAKE YOUR OWN GIFT WRAP:

- OLD POSTERS
- REUSABLE TINS OR BASKETS
- OLD CALENDARS
- NEWSPAPER COMICS
- SHEET MUSIC
- REPORT CARDS OR ESSAYS
- COLOURING BOOK PAGES
- OLD MAPS
- CEREAL BOXES
- OLD WRAPPING PAPER

DON'T GO FOR ALL THOSE RIBBONS AND BOWS! USE:

- VCR/CASSETTE RIBBON
- SILK SCARVES
- PINE CONES OR TWIGS
- HEMP TWINE
- FABRIC SCRAPS
- DRIED FLOWERS

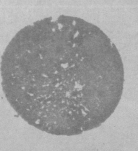
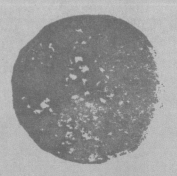

If You love this planet

Meet Your Eco Footprint

To become a better friend to the planet, you first have to know what effect your actions have on the Earth. A few years ago, Canadian scientists developed a way for us to see what our individual impact is on the environment.

Your ecological footprint, or eco footprint, measures how much of the Earth's resources you use, along with how long it takes for the planet to absorb what you waste.

Your eco footprint gives you an idea of how all your daily decisions impact the environment. It's like a report card — you find out what you're really good at and what you can improve on. Once you understand how your choices affect the Earth, it's even easier to get moving and save the planet!

It's called a **footprint** because **all** our actions leave **something** behind.

To-do List

Simple, everyday choices can help keep your eco footprint low!

- Use reusable containers for lunch
- Eat a few meat-free meals a week
- Take short showers, not baths
- Avoid buying things with lots of unnecessary packaging
- Turn your computer off when you're not using it
- Help your parents shop green: buy locally-grown food whenever possible
- Walk to school
- Carpool to soccer practice

Balance of Power

Scientists say that carbon dioxide (CO_2) is the main cause of global warming, the gradual rise in the Earth's temperature. As more CO_2 and other greenhouse gases build up in the Earth's atmosphere, more heat is trapped on the Earth's surface.

Why is so much CO_2 being produced? Well, almost everything we do requires energy from fossil fuels, such as oil, coal, and natural gas. Turning on a light switch. Driving a car. Eating a fast-food meal. These things all release CO_2 into the atmosphere.

The easiest thing we can all do to reduce our eco footprint is to be more efficient when using fossil fuels. Also, we can consider using renewable energy sources, such as solar power or wind turbines.

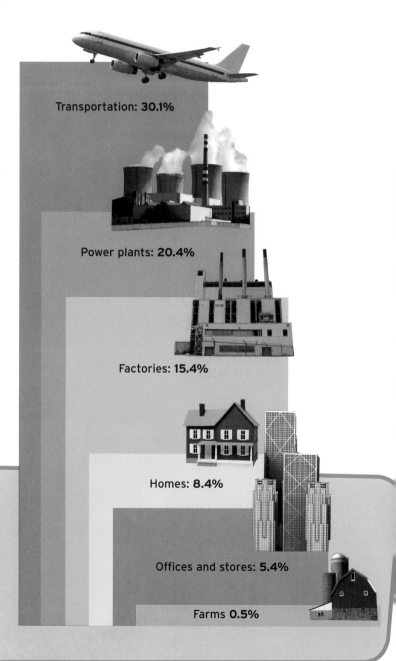

Transportation: 30.1%

Power plants: 20.4%

Factories: 15.4%

Homes: 8.4%

Offices and stores: 5.4%

Farms 0.5%

Energy Zappers
The top energy consumers in Canada

So where does all of our power go and who uses it? Here are our country's biggest energy eaters.

What Else Goes in Your Footprint?

Your eco footprint is determined by many factors. (Hint: Think about which activities emit a lot of carbon dioxide and which ones emit less.)

 Home: You have the power to use electricity wisely. Be careful with the energy use in your family's home. The less time you spend using kitchen appliances, watching TV, and using water, the smaller your footprint will be.

 Food: Your food choices are all connected to the Earth. It takes a lot of energy to grow crops and raise animals for eating. Most of our food travels a long distance before it reaches our plates. But if you buy food from local farms, it has less of an impact on the planet.

 Transportation: How you get around is important. Walking or riding your bike is Earth-friendly. Vehicles need gasoline to run, which releases tons of carbon dioxide into the atmosphere. Carpooling and taking the bus can help take cars off the road – and points off your footprint.

 Waste: Everything you throw out affects the planet. Most landfills just bury trash over and over again. Reusing and recycling keeps stuff out of the landfill, and composting returns resources to the soil. Remember this: your trash has to go somewhere – so try not to make too much!

Did you know?

Throwing something out is just like leaving the lights on in an empty room — both actions waste energy!

The Big and the Small

Who has the biggest footprint worldwide? The answer may surprise you.

The biggest eco footprints in the world belong to developed nations. According to the World Wildlife Federation, the United Arab Emirates (U.A.E.) has the world's biggest footprint. Other developed countries like Canada and the U.S. are not far behind the U.A.E. These nations spend lots of money on fossil fuels to heat and cool homes, power cars, and fuel planes.

The smallest ecological footprints belong to developing nations. Many African countries have small footprints because people there don't spend as much on things like food or fuel. For example, in Somalia, most people don't have home electricity or cars to drive. Many of them grow their own food. Developing nations use far less than their share of Earth's resources.

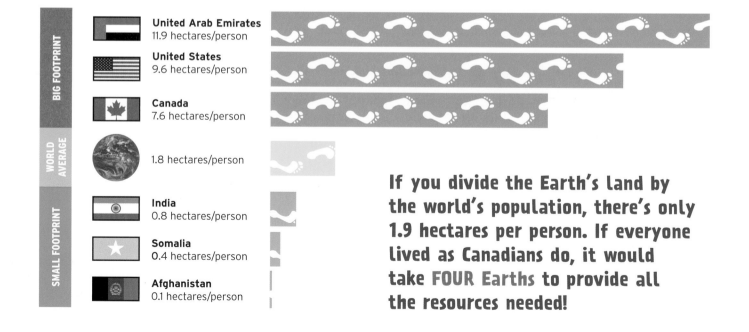

BIG FOOTPRINT

United Arab Emirates
11.9 hectares/person

United States
9.6 hectares/person

Canada
7.6 hectares/person

WORLD AVERAGE

1.8 hectares/person

SMALL FOOTPRINT

India
0.8 hectares/person

Somalia
0.4 hectares/person

Afghanistan
0.1 hectares/person

If you divide the Earth's land by the world's population, there's only 1.9 hectares per person. If everyone lived as Canadians do, it would take FOUR Earths to provide all the resources needed!

Quiz Yourself

Want to know where you fit on the footprint scale? Take this quick quiz to find out!

Check out Zerofootprint Kids Calculator for more info!
www.zerofootprintkids.com

1 How do you get to school most days?
 a) car
 b) bus
 c) walk or bike

2 How often do you eat meat products?
 a) every day
 b) once or twice a week
 c) never, I'm a vegetarian

3 How many bags of garbage does your family produce each week?
 a) three or more
 b) two
 c) one

4 What is your favourite after-school activity?
 a) getting your parents to drive you to the mall for some shopping
 b) surfing the net
 c) reading a book

5 Do you turn off the lights when you leave a room?
 a) no, someone else will do it
 b) sometimes, if I remember
 c) always

MOSTLY A's:
BIG FOOTPRINT
Don't be discouraged! There's still time to make a difference.

MOSTLY B's:
MEDIUM FOOTPRINT
On the right track. Try harder to remember the little things.

MOSTLY C's:
SMALL FOOTPRINT
Great job! Pat yourself on the back and keep it up.

Shout Out

"A lot of kids think that saving the Earth is an adult's job, but kids can help the Earth just as much as adults can."

Larissa Kubitz, 11

Together, we can make a difference.

Shelby Dickey, 13

"We need to make our Earth healthy and keep it that way!"

Alexa Hewson, 11

"Adults have the power to encourage the younger generation to help global warming!"

Greta Whipple, 12

> **If everybody on the Earth picked up at least one piece of garbage a day, there would be over 6 billion pieces of garbage picked up each day.**
>
> Jason Field, 13

> Write to politicians, talk to whoever will listen, and raise awareness about the environment before it's too late!
>
> Allie Grady, 14

> **Even the smallest actions add up, contributing to a 'greener' planet.**
>
> Rachel Stadder, 13

What do YOU think we can do to help our planet?

Eco All-stars

Meet some enviro-activists who are doing their part to save the planet

Stop Your Engines!

Who:

Anna Talman, a 9-year-old from Edmonton, Alberta

What She Did:

Anna started up an organization named ECO-AIR (Edmonton's Children-Organized Anti-Idling Recruiters). The group is trying to put an end to car idling — that's when people leave their car and truck engines running while they're waiting around in driveways, outside schools, or in parking lots. Leaving an engine running for no reason is a waste of fuel and causes pollution. Anna went to the Edmonton city council two times to try to get a law passed that would ban idling.

Why She Did It:

Anna was downtown one day and saw a car idling. When she found it hard to breathe, she knew idling was a problem. She founded ECO-AIR so she could change her neighbourhood.

What Happened:

City council didn't pass the anti-idling law. But there's still great news for Anna and ECO-AIR. City officials are planning to print ads, brochures, and signs reminding motorists about the harm of leaving their cars running.

What's Next:

The council's ad campaign is still in the works. And Anna says she won't give up on trying to get the anti-idling law passed.

Fuel Up!

Who:
Steven Henderson, a 16-year-old from Ponteland, Northumberland, England

What He Did:
Steven began making biodiesel in his family's barn. Biodiesel is a natural fuel that produces less CO_2 when it's burned than fuels such as coal and oil. Steven collects used vegetable oil from local restaurant kitchens and then transforms it into biodiesel on weekends.

Why He Did It:
Steven's father bought him a book about global warming. After reading the book and studying climate change at school, he decided he needed to do something to help the planet. That's when he told his dad that he wanted to make biodiesel.

What's Next:
Steven is now working on a way to use the biodiesel to provide heat and electricity for his family's house!

What Happened:
Not only did Steven begin making biodiesel, but he made enough to power his father's farm equipment. And it gets better. This green fuel is saving his father the money that he used to spend on gas for his vehicles. All that, and it's helping out the planet, too!

A Bright Idea

Who:
Avery Hairston, a 15-year-old from New York City, New York

What He Did:
Avery started up a charity called RelightNY to educate people in New York City about switching from regular light bulbs to compact fluorescent light bulbs (CFLs). A CFL uses 75 percent less energy than a regular bulb and lasts 10 times longer. The charity also gives away CFLs to families who can't afford them.

Why He Did It:
Avery saw a newspaper ad about how CFLs can help stop global warming. After thinking it over, he came up with the idea for his enviro-friendly charity.

What Happened:
Through donations, RelightNY has raised more than $70,000. And it has supplied 3,000 bulbs to families who couldn't afford them otherwise.

What's Next:
For now, Avery's charity is focusing on educating the people of his community in New York City. But he hopes to one day set the charity up in other cities throughout the United States.

School Daze

You ask your parents to drive you to school... but it's only two blocks away.
GO BACK TO START

Lunch Break

You bring your lunch in reusable containers. No garbage!
MOVE 1 SPACE FORWARD

Brush Up

You turn off the tap while brushing your teeth.
MOVE 1 SPACE FORWARD

Everyday Actions

How do our daily choices affect the planet? Play this quick game to find out!

Field Trip

Your class goes to a local forest to learn about planting trees. Then you help plant one.
MOVE 2 SPACES FORWARD

E-waste

You buy a new computer but your old one works just fine. The old computer gets kicked to the curb.
MOVE 2 SPACES BACK

START HERE

To play:

1. Place a button on the **START** space to mark your place and roll a die to begin.

2. When you stop on a square, follow the instructions.

3. The first one to reach the finish line is crowned **green**-ius!

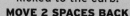

What's for Dinner?

Your food has travelled from different parts of the world to get to your dinner plate, racking up thousands of food miles.

MOVE 1 SPACE BACK

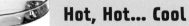

Hot, Hot... Cool

Whoa, it's a scorcher out there! Instead of cranking the air conditioner, you settle for an ice-cold glass of tap water.

MOVE 1 SPACE FORWARD

YOU RULE!

Way to go, green-ius! The world is greener thanks to your environmentally friendly choices.

Trash Time

Your parents ask you to take out the garbage. To save time, you throw the recyclables and compost into one big trash bag.

MOVE 4 SPACES BACK

Play It Again

Your older sister gives you her old baseball glove so you can practise for tryouts.

MOVE 1 SPACE FORWARD

Turn It Off

Before bedtime, you notice the family computer is on standby. You turn off the computer and flick off the power bar, too.

MOVE 1 SPACE FORWARD

Small **actions,** **big results**

CHEW ON THIS
SLOW FOOD = SMART FOOD

FAST FOOD MAY INDEED BE QUICK,
BUT ON THE ROAD TO HEALTHY EATING,
SLOW AND STEADY WINS THE RACE.

FAST FOOD IS
A DOWNER. ALL
THAT FAT, SUGAR,
AND SALT CAN
TAKE A TOLL ON
YOUR BODY.

SLOW FOOD IS
ABOUT TAKING YOUR TIME.
IT'S WORTH THE EFFORT
TO MAKE HEALTHY MEALS.

make your next meal
a party! you can work
with friends on your
delectable dinners.

buying local produce
is the first step
to greener meals.
check out the fruits,
vegetables, meat
and dairy products
grown just around
the corner.

pick up a
cookbook or two
to get started
on your tasty
adventure

WHAT YOU'LL NEED

- ➤ tomato seedling
- ➤ green pepper seedling
- ➤ basil seeds

- ➤ gardening soil
- ➤ mulch
- ➤ metre-high stick

- ➤ twine or string
- ➤ small planting pot
- ➤ watering can

Plant a Pizza

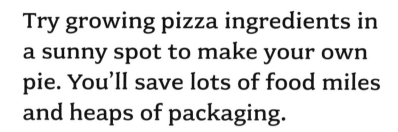

Try growing pizza ingredients in a sunny spot to make your own pie. You'll save lots of food miles and heaps of packaging.

Okay, so you can't actually grow your own pizza in a garden, but if you follow these instructions, in a few months you'll sprout your own delicious toppings. Be sure to plant these ingredients in a sunny area. Then try the recipe on page 59 to make an awesome pizza dough. As for the cheese, unless you have your own cow, you gotta grab that at your local market.

TIP: If you don't have a backyard, grow your toppings in pots on your balcony or windowsill.

Tomatoes

- Dig a hole for the seedling's roots. Press soil around the plant so that only the vine peeks out.
- Push a stick into the soil beside the seedling. Loosely tie the seedling to the stick to hold it upright.
- Water your plant whenever the soil feels dry just beneath the surface.
- When the tomatoes have turned red, they're ready to be eaten. Don't forget to wash them first!

By making your own homemade pizza you save:	
1 cardboard pizza box	1 delivery driver's gas
1 plastic pizza box holder	1 paper receipt

Green Peppers

- Dig a hole for the seedling's roots. Pat soil firmly around the seedling, and surround it with mulch (such as cut grass or fallen leaves) to keep the roots moist and weeds away.
- Water the pepper plant whenever the soil feels dry just beneath the surface.
- When the peppers are at least the size of a tennis ball, they're ready to eat. Cut them off with scissors – pulling will hurt the plant.

Basil

- Fill a pot with soil, leaving a bit of room at the top edge.
- Dig small holes in the soil and put a seed in each hole. Lightly cover seeds with soil.
- Water only as needed. Herbs like basil do not need much water, so make sure the soil is only slightly wet.
- When clusters of leaves start to appear, they are ready to eat. Pick basil leaves in the morning before the sun dries out their oils.
- Always leave a few leaves near the stem's base. This way more leaves will grow. If you see flower buds appear on the plant, pick them off. They take away from the plant's growing power.

WHAT YOU'LL NEED

- pizza dough (store-bought, or make your own with the recipe on page 59)
- flour
- rolling pin
- pizza pan

Trusty Crust

Flipping and rolling your own pizza dough takes some practice, but it's also a lot of fun. Check out these handy tips, and soon you'll be tossing your dough like a pro!

1 Place a ball of dough in a handful of flour. Then smash it down with the palm of your hand to flatten it.

2 Stretch the dough out or roll it with a rolling pin until it's about the size of a dinner plate.

Slap it back and forth between your hands to remove the excess flour.

Hold the dough flat in your hands and toss it up in the air, spinning it clockwise or counter-clockwise.

If you threw the dough clockwise, hold it on the palm of your left hand. With your right hand, make a fist. (If you threw it counter-clockwise, use the opposite hands.)

Push your palm up, rotating it back and forth. Then toss the dough up into the air.

Catch the pizza dough with both fists. Then quickly toss it up again the same way. (Hint: The faster you can go, the bigger your dough will get.)

Always keep your hands under the outside edges of the dough. Keep on tossing your pizza dough until it's the size you want.

- ➤ pizza dough (store-bought, or use the recipe below)
- ➤ pizza sauce
- ➤ grated mozzarella cheese
- ➤ your choice of toppings
- ➤ pizza pan or baking sheet

FORGET DELIVERY! • PROJECT 17 • MAKE YOUR OWN PIZZA

'Za-di-dah

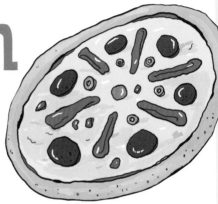

Sink your teeth into homemade pizza, fresh from the oven.

1 Toss the dough (see page 56). Place it on a lightly greased pizza pan.

2 Spread a layer of pizza sauce over the dough so it's about 1 cm (0.5 in.) from the edges.

3 Add handfuls of your favourite toppings, spreading them evenly around the pizza. Top it all with grated mozzarella cheese.

4 Bake at 220°C (425°F) for 25 minutes, or until the crust is golden. Slice and enjoy.

You're the Tops

Here are some classic pizza-topping ideas:
- sliced tomatoes
- chopped green or red pepper
- chopped basil
- sliced mushrooms
- chopped ham, bacon, or chicken
- pineapple tidbits
- chopped spinach
- chopped red onion
- feta cheese
- or come up with your own unique toppings

Pizza Dough

You'll need:

500 mL (2 cups) flour

8 g (1/4 oz.) instant dried yeast

5 mL (1 tsp.) sugar

2 mL (1/2 tsp.) salt

15 mL (1 tbsp.) olive oil

250 mL (1 cup) warm water

What to do:

1. Sift the flour, yeast, sugar, and salt together in a large bowl. Stir in the oil, then slowly add the water to make a soft dough. You might not need all of the water, so add only a little at a time!

2. Lightly flour your hands and work surface. Knead the dough until it becomes smooth and stretchy, about 10 minutes.

3. Roll the dough into a ball, place in a lightly greased bowl, and cover. Let the dough rest in a warm place for about an hour, until it doubles in size. You're ready to toss!

swap UNTIL YOU DROP

TRADE OLD CLOTHES AMONG FRIENDS FOR A BRAND-NEW WARDROBE.

GIVE YOUR CDS, DVDS, AND VIDEO GAMES A NEW SPIN BY STARTING A SWAP.

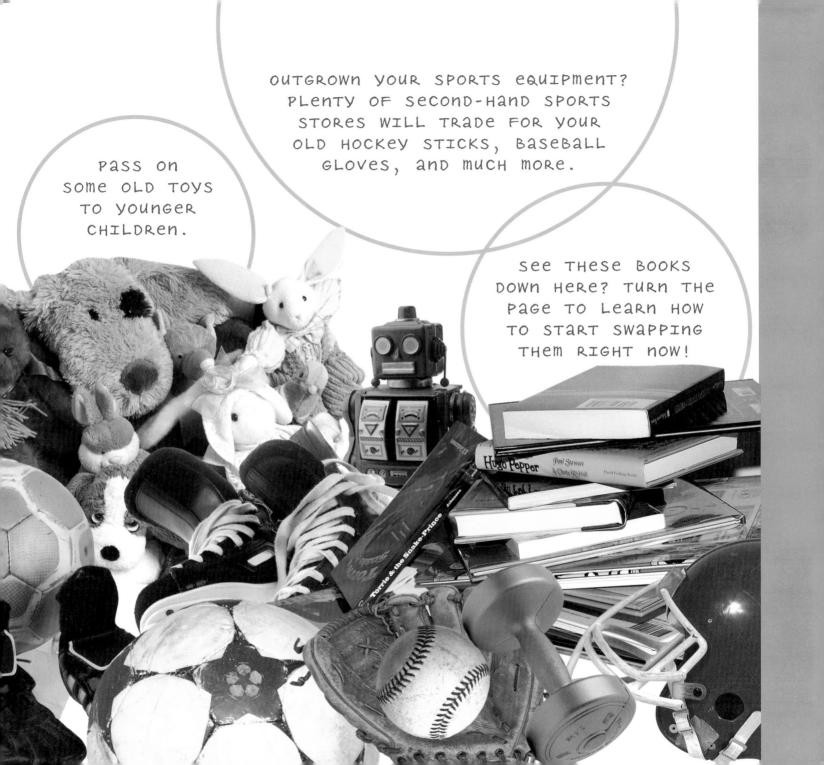

OUTGROWN YOUR SPORTS EQUIPMENT?
PLENTY OF SECOND-HAND SPORTS
STORES WILL TRADE FOR YOUR
OLD HOCKEY STICKS, BASEBALL
GLOVES, AND MUCH MORE.

PASS ON
SOME OLD TOYS
TO YOUNGER
CHILDREN.

SEE THESE BOOKS
DOWN HERE? TURN THE
PAGE TO LEARN HOW
TO START SWAPPING
THEM RIGHT NOW!

WHAT YOU'LL NEED

➤ scrap paper or cardboard (for invitations and tickets)
➤ pens or markers
➤ books
➤ table
➤ hat or bag

Swap Meet

Is your shelf piling up with old books you no longer read? Get some friends together and trade those titles for new ones.

You are invited to a Book Swap

Where _____
when _____
to bring _____

1 Send handmade invitations to friends for your swap. Write the swap's date, time, and your address on pieces of paper or cardboard made to look like bookmarks. Tell your friends the more books they bring, the more they'll take home. If you'd like to save paper, you can email your invitations instead.

TIP: You can swap all kinds of things. Use these pages as a guide for setting up swaps for clothing, sporting goods, CDs, toys – there's no limit to what you can trade.

Things That Go BOOM!

Nature: Gone Wild!

Pro Soccer Tips – Kick It!

Paper, Rock and Scissors

Peter, The Pumpkin, and The Princess

Look out, Wilbur Prescott!

THE UNDEFINABLE DEEDS OF MS. MABLE MUSTARD

The **BIG** Book of Unknown Mysteries

Science! – an introductory encyclopedia

The Fiery Mountain

Historical Achievements: How They Did It

At the End of White Birch Road

ple Syrup and Me: A Fun Guide to Can

2 As your friends arrive to the swap, hand out one ticket for each book they bring. Then place the books on a table so everyone can check out the goods.

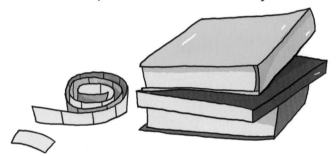

3 To decide the order guests choose their books, put numbered slips of paper into a hat or bag and have everyone draw one without looking.

4 Have the person who drew number one browse the swap spot and select a book. One ticket is good for one book. Then the second person chooses a book and so on. Make sure everybody has a turn before people with more tickets go up.

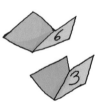

Did you know?

Trees are nature's air purifiers. They remove CO_2 from the atmosphere and replace it with oxygen — the very same oxygen that we need to breathe! By swapping, you're helping save a few of those trees from being turned into unneeded extra books.

5 Keep a pad of sticky notes on hand. If people want to read a book they didn't get, write their names on a sticky note inside the book so they can borrow it later! Donate leftover books to a hospital, charity, or school library.

Why not play a game too?

Write some of the book titles on strips of paper. Divide your friends into two teams. Then have them pull a title out of a hat. Each person tries to get his or her own team to guess the title by drawing it on an easel or whiteboard.

WITH a BASKET, BAGS, OR RACK, YOU CaN CARRY aLL SORTS OF THINGS ON YOUR BIKE.

WHY BIKES RULE...

IT'S GREAT FUN RACING BIKES WITH FRIENDS.

CYCLING IS a QUICK aND EaSY WaY TO ZIP aROUND TOWN. NO TRaFFIC JaMS FOR YOU!

BIKES ARE THE ULTIMATE GREEN MACHINE — YOUR LEGS ARE YOUR ENGINE!

BIKES ARE CHEAP AND EASY TO FIX.

SLAPPING SOME STICKERS ON YOUR BIKE CAN MAKE IT LIKE NO OTHER.

A HELMET CAN COVER UP YOUR BAD HAIR DAY.

BIKING IS NOT ONLY FUN, IT'S PRETTY HEALTHY TOO — JUST DON'T TELL ANYONE!

GET YOUR BIKE

PROJECT **19**

READY TO ROLL

WHAT YOU'LL NEED TO CARE FOR YOUR BIKE

- cloth
- bicycle oil
- bicycle pump
- Allen key
- adjustable wrench
- screwdriver

Road Ready

With a few simple tools and a bit of know-how, you'll be able to keep your bike rolling safely all year long.

Your Tool Box

cloth

bicycle oil

bicycle pump

Allen key

adjustable wrench

screwdriver

WHAT YOU'LL NEED WHEN YOU ARE OUT ON THE ROAD

- ➤ helmet
- ➤ tire pump
- ➤ tire patch kit
- ➤ bike lock
- ➤ tool and safety kit
- ➤ water
- ➤ granola bars or other high-energy snack

Meet Your Bike

bell

brake and gear cables

brakes

tool and safety kit

gears

brake pads

frame

tire

spokes

water bottle

reflector

chain

pedals

rims

69

A Perfect Fit

Getting Started

Make sure your bike fits you. Sit on your seat and check that the leg on the lower pedal is almost straight. Your other foot should be flat on the ground. If it's not, ask an adult to help adjust the height of your seat.

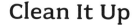

Wear sneakers when you cycle. Sandals or bare feet make it difficult to grip the pedals.

Clean It Up

Cleaning your bike regularly keeps it running smoothly. Wipe down the frame, pedals, brakes, tires, and rims with a damp cloth.

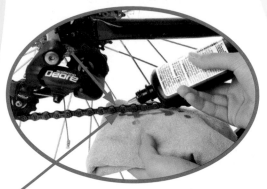

Lightly apply bike oil along the inside and outside of the chain. (Use a cloth to catch drips.) Leave the oil on for a few minutes, then gently wipe off excess with the cloth.

Nuts and Bolts

Shake, Rattle, and Roll

Lift your bike a few inches off the ground and let it bounce. Look for any loose parts and tighten them with a screwdriver or Allen key.

Check pedals for wobbling. If they're loose, tighten the bolt with a wrench.

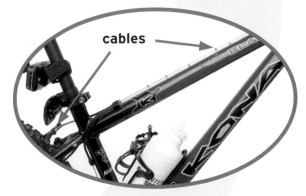

cables

Examine the brake and gear cables for any fraying. If frayed, go to a bike shop to have them replaced.

Take a short ride to check that your gears switch easily. If they don't, get them fixed by a pro.

Make sure your water bottle holder is securely attached. If it wobbles or rattles, tighten its screws.

Wheel It Out

Check for flat tires by squeezing them with your hands. Pump them with air for a smoother, safer ride.

squeeze here

Check that all of the reflectors on your bike are securely attached. If not, tighten them with a screwdriver.

Check that your brake pads are secure. Look for any wear. If the pads are loose or worn down all the way, take your bike to a repair shop.

Head Case

Make sure your helmet fits properly

Check your helmet for cracks. If your helmet ever hit the ground in a fall, you should replace it. The protective foam inside could be cracked—and that means it won't keep your noggin safe if you fall.

 Right way
Fits snugly and sits evenly on head.

 Wrong way
Tips back or forward and strap is loose.

Safety First

Always remember to...

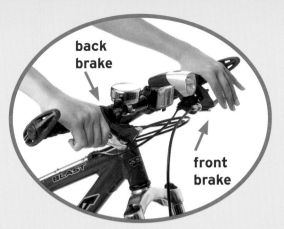

back brake

front brake

- **Wear your helmet** making sure it fits properly.

- **Stay alert!** Watch out for things that are in your path, like loose gravel or broken glass.

- **Dress properly** by wearing light-coloured clothes so you're easy to spot. Don't wear baggy pants that can get caught in a bike's moving parts.

- **Obey all signs**, signals, and rules of the road, no matter where you're riding.

- **Ride in single file** when cycling with friends.

- **Be prepared** on long rides. Bring along your wrench set, tire pump, patch kit, and bike lock, as well as a water bottle and healthy snacks.

- **Use your brakes properly.** If you have hand brakes, stop by squeezing the back brake slightly before squeezing the front one.

- **Test your bell** to make sure it works. If it's loose, tighten the screws with a screwdriver.

- **Listen!** Don't bring your MP3 player along for the ride. You need to hear everything around you when biking.

73

Your green guide

Talk
like a
Climate-
change
Expert

Your Green Term Glossary

Biodegradable

Items that will eventually break down safely if left in a natural environment.

BIOLOGICAL DIVERSITY OR BIODIVERSITY

The variety of life forms that live within an ecosystem. Scientists use biodiversity to measure the health of an area.

Carbon neutral

Any project that balances the amount of carbon dioxide it produces with an act that removes an equal amount of carbon from the atmosphere. This is usually done by planting trees to remove carbon dioxide from the air.

Clear-cutting

The forestry practice of removing a very large area of trees all at once.

Carbon footprint

The amount of carbon dioxide released into the atmosphere as a result of one's daily activities, such as driving, food miles, or use of household appliances.

COMPOST

Allowing organic waste, such as food, paper, and yard waste, to decompose naturally. This decomposed material provides excellent minerals for gardens.

Ecosystem

A natural, interdependent grouping of animals, plants, fungi, and/or micro-organisms. A rise or fall in the number of one member of this group affects the other members.

Fossil fuels

Sources of burnable energy that have formed over millions of years under the Earth's surface, such as coal. They are made of the remains of ancient animals and plants.

ENDANGERED SPECIES

Any type of animal or plant at risk of becoming extinct, or disappearing forever.

Greenhouse gases

Pollutants in the Earth's atmosphere that trap the sun's heat around the planet. These gases include carbon dioxide, methane, and nitrous oxide.

Food miles

The distance that food has travelled to arrive at your home, especially from other countries or continents.

Landfill

An area where garbage materials are dumped, piled, and eventually covered by soil and dirt.

Organic

Animal and plant products that are grown without the use of chemicals. It's 100 percent naturally raised food.

SOLAR PANEL

A flat device used to collect sunlight and turn it into energy.

Sustainable communities

A city or town that is able to function indefinitely without draining or polluting its environment of food, water, and energy.

PUBLIC TRANSIT

A system of vehicles, such as buses, subways, or streetcars, that are used to transport a city's people.

Wind farm

An area where a large number of wind turbines have been built to provide renewable energy.

Renewable energy

Any type of power that does not destroy its source to create energy. Wind, solar, and hydro power are all types of renewable energy — in theory, these sources will never run out!

Zero emissions

Describing any appliance or vehicle that runs without producing exhaust of any kind.

Listen UP

Everybody's weighing in on the environment.

" We can be environmentalists. So get educated. Stay educated. So we can think for ourselves. And join the fight to save this unique blue planet for future generations. "

Leonardo DiCaprio, actor and environmental activist

Our survival depends on abandoning conflict, working for peace, sharing what we have, and living within our ecological means.

Elizabeth May, leader of Canada's Green Party

> " If [people] just changed one aspect of their life, if they just did one thing differently, that alone is a step closer to solving the problem... This problem can be solved. "

Cameron Diaz, actor

> " Green to me is just an exciting, exciting term for the future...There's a lot to do and a lot of people are doing a lot of exciting stuff for the environment.

Ben Harper, musician

> " We should start thinking about the way we live and the impact it has on the world. "

David Suzuki, environmental activist

> " I'm under no illusions about how big an impact one person can make. But I do think that if all of us begin to make these changes, it adds up. "

Al Gore, Chairman of the Alliance for Climate Protection and star of the documentary film *An Inconvenient Truth*

Who inspires YOU to care about the environment?

What's Your ECO-IQ?

Think you're so green you should have roots? Take this enviro-quiz and find out the facts on the green scene.

1. T F You'll save more water by taking a bath instead of a shower.

2. T F If you leave a charger plugged in after you remove your cellphone or MP3 player, it still uses energy.

3. T F The only way for you and your family to create less waste is to recycle.

4. T F You can help out the planet by riding your bike to school.

5. T F Uneaten food scraps, like vegetable peelings and eggshells, can be turned into a soil-like product called compost.

6. T F There's not much you can do to make eating out more enviro-friendly.

7 T F Changing a light bulb in your desk lamp is good for the planet.

8 T F When you go to the grocery store with your family, it's best to choose paper bags over plastic ones.

9 T F You should throw used-up batteries in the garbage.

Answers

1. **False.** It can take a lot of water to fill the average bathtub. You'll use about one-third the water by washing up in a quick shower.

2. **True.** A charger sucks up energy even when nothing is plugged into it. The wasted electricity is called phantom power. Lots of household items, including TVs, computers, and stereos use phantom power because they're always plugged in.

3. **False.** Recycling rocks, but reducing is tops. If we reduce the amount of garbage we create, it'll mean less trash in our landfills. Try buying products that have little or no packaging.

4. **True.** Cars release a lot of CO_2 into the air. To give the planet a CO_2 break, you can also try walking, boarding, or giving your scooter a whirl.

5. **True.** About 30 percent of your family's home waste can be composted. By composting, you'll cut down on what your family throws out and give nutrients back to the Earth.

6. **False.** Try to avoid take-out food. All those wrappers, containers, cups, and straws add up to a mountain of garbage.

7. **True.** Replacing a regular bulb with a compact fluorescent light bulb (CFL) is a bright idea. It uses 75 percent less energy and lasts 10 times longer than a regular bulb.

8. **False.** Both paper and plastic bags are bad for our environment. The solution? Use an eco-friendly canvas bag!

9. **False.** Batteries contain hazardous metals that can end up hurting the environment. Take them to a nearby hazardous waste depot. Better yet, try to use rechargeable or recycled batteries, or buy things that don't need batteries at all!

What's Your Score?
8 or 9 right	You're an eco all-star
6 to 7 right	Welcome to the enviro-team
5 or fewer right	Get with the green scene

Site-seeing

A quick green guide to the web

Facts and Challenges

www.ecokids.ca
EcoKids is full of games, facts, and interactive questions about how easy it can be to become green. Find out what kids just like you are doing to protect the environment.

www.davidsuzuki.org/kids
David Suzuki has been speaking out about the environment since before you were born. So are you ready to be put to his test? Take his challenge and become a better friend to the planet.

www.epa.gov/highschool
Everything around you — the air, water, plants, animals, soil — is affected by pollution and climate change. This website from the EPA, or Environmental Protection Agency, is packed with facts and articles to improve your eco-education!

www.zerofootprintkids.com
This website helps you calculate your own carbon footprint. Answer questions to learn how much carbon you're producing. Compare your personal score with averages from around the world and get tips on how to lower your number.

www.kidsplanet.org/factsheets/map.html
Many animals around the world are threatened by pollution, climate change, and overhunting. See a list of endangered animals and find out what you can do to help keep them alive and thriving.

Food and Health

www.kidsregen.org
Growing your own food helps more than just the environment — it keeps you healthy too! Learn how to plant, grow, and cook your own food.

www.edibleschoolyard.org
The students at Martin Luther King Jr. Middle School actually made their own organic garden. Learn how students and teachers have worked together to provide healthy food for themselves.

Get Active!

teenink.com/Environment
Tired of listening to adults talk about the environment? At Teen Ink, teens write about their concerns and offer solutions on eating right and living green. Pick from a large library of student essays, or even submit something that you've written!

www.kidsface.org
The world's a big place to try to save all at once. KidsFACE stands for Kids for a Clean Environment. This online youth community helps to organize kids all over the world to plant trees, write letters to their governments, and much more.

teensforplanetearth.org
This site has everything for teenagers to begin their quest to help the Earth, including a resource library, contests, regular news, and even information on future careers helping the planet. Think you'd like to make saving the Earth your full-time job? This isn't a bad place to start!

Green
in any language

1. ⊃ᵖᒥᐧᖅ ᑦ ᓇ ᓯᑦ
2. vihreä
3. grün
4. خضر
5. हरा
6. kākāriki
7. gwyrdd
8. vert
9. zöld
10. kijani
11. πράσινο
12. verde

13 maintso

14 초록색

15 berde

16 roheline

17 зелёный

18 ירוק

19 hijau

20 绿色

21 ʻOmaʻomaʻo

22 Zielony

23 grøn

24 yeşil

25 สีเขียว

26 green

LANGUAGES:

1. Inuktitut
2. Finnish
3. German
4. Arabic
5. Hindi
6. Maori
7. Welsh
8. French
9. Hungarian
10. Swahili
11. Greek
12. Italian, Portuguese, Spanish
13. Malagasy
14. Korean
15. Tagalog
16. Estonian
17. Russian
18. Hebrew
19. Indonesian
20. Chinese
21. Hawaiian
22. Polish
23. Danish
24. Turkish
25. Thai
26. English

Go Team!

The OWL Magazine staff lets you in on their favourite (green) things!

My favourite green activity is watering the plant by my desk at OWL. It's a jade plant. Named Jay.
Craig Battle, Editor

If I could make one green change to my city, I'd add more rooftop gardens!
Jackie Farquhar, D.I.Y. Editor

Selected Bibliography

Books

Cheel, Richard. *Global Warming Alert! (Disaster Alert!).* Crabtree Publishing Company, 2007.

David, Laurie, and Cambria Gordon. *The Down-to-Earth Guide to Global Warming.* Orchard Books, 2007.

Degler, Teri, and Dennis Lee. *The Canadian Junior Green Guide.* McClelland and Stewart Inc., 1990.

De Rothschild, David. *The Live Earth Global Warming Survival Handbook.* Rodale Books, 2007.

Hough, Rich. *You Can Save the Planet: A Day in the Life of Your Carbon Footprint.* A & C Black Publishers Ltd., 2007.

Leslie, Jeremy, and David Roberts. *Pick Me Up.* DK Children, 2007.

Morris, Neil. *Global Warming (What If We Do Nothing?).* World Almanac Library, 2007.

Thornhill, Jan. *This Is My Planet: The Kids' Guide to Global Warming.* Maple Tree Press Inc., 2007.

Yarrow, Joanna. *1,001 Ways to Save the Earth.* Chronicle Books, 2007.

Websites

AutoBlogGreen. www.autobloggreen.com

Captain Planet Foundation. www.captainplanetfdn.org

CBC News: Climate Change. www.cbc.ca/news/background/kyoto/climatechange.html

Chronicle Live: Talented Teen Transforms Cooking Oil into Fuel. www.chroniclelive.co.uk/north-east-news/todays-evening-chronicle/2006/12/09/talented-teen-transforms-cooking-oil-into-fuel-72703-18236640/

CNN.com: Global Hot Spots. edition.cnn.com/SPECIALS/2005/changing.earth/

Composting Council of Canada. www.compost.org

David Suzuki Foundation. www.davidsuzuki.org

Eartheasy. eartheasy.com

Earth Rangers. www.earthrangers.ca

Earth Share of Washington: Pact Reached to Turn Gas from Landfill into Energy.
www.esw.org/news/archives/2007/07/pact_reached_to_turn_gas_from.php

EcoKids. www.ecokids.ca

Edmonton Journal: Ad Campaign Targets Idling Vehicles.
www.canada.com/edmontonjournal/news/cityplus/story.html?id=8edb3ef3-2105-4bea-af77-e01dbd5c59e8

Environment Canada. www.ec.gc.ca

Friends of the Earth. www.foe.org/globalwarming

GM FYI Blog: One Man's Garbage Is... fyi.gmblogs.com/2006/04/one_mans_garbage_is.html

Green Belt Movement. greenbeltmovement.org

Greenpeace. www.greenpeace.org

How Stuff Works: How Global Warming Works. science.howstuffworks.com/global-warming

Live Science: How You Can Fight Global Warming. www.livescience.com/environment

Media News Today: Key to Win-Win Global Warming Solution Is Reducing Tropical Deforestation In Brazil.
www.medicalnewstoday.com/articles/71109.php

People and Planet. www.planetfriendly.net

RelightNY. www.relightny.com

Stop Global Warming.org. www.stopglobalwarming.org

Treehugger. www.treehugger.com

United States Environmental Protection Agency: Climate Change Kids Site.
epa.gov/climatechange/kids

USA Today: Climate Report Predicts Deadly Heat Waves, Flooding in Europe.
www.usatoday.com/weather/climate/globalwarming/2007-04-11-europe-prediction_N.htm

Vanityfair.com: Fifty Ways to Help Save the Planet.
www.vanityfair.com/politics/features/2006/05/savetheplanet200605

Zerofootprint. http://www.zerofootprintkids.com

Index

Credits

Consultants

Special thanks to Diana Suzuki, Earth Day Canada; Geoff Coulson, Environment Canada; Jacinthe Lacroix, Environment Canada; Sharon Philpott, Environment Canada; Mark Cullen, markcullen.com; Ken Baldwin, Natural Resources Canada; Valerie Thom, Pitch-in Canada; Elizabeth Everhardus, Pollution Probe; Trees Ontario; William Rees, University of British Columbia; Gene Arganosa, University of Saskatchewan

Illustrators

Michael Cho: 56-58
Aaron Leighton: cover, 1, 3, 4, 5, 6, 7, 8, 9, 34, 35, 36, 44, 50, 51, 54, 74, 75, 76, 78, 79, 86, 87, 90, 91, 92, 93, 96
Monika Melnychuk: 12, 13, 15, 17, 18, 19, 20, 22, 28, 29, 59, 62, 64, 65, 68, 73
Ryan Price: 66-67, 82, 83

Writers

Maria Birmingham: 44-47, 56-58, 82-83
John Crossingham: 76-79, 84-85
Mandy Ng: 36-41, 48-49

Photos

Monica McKenna: 7, 92 (Jackie Farquhar)
Chris Gonzaga: 12, 16, 63
Hal Roth: 15, 17, 18, 19, 22, 23, 27, back cover (T-shirt, bag)
Angela Pilas-Magee: 20, 21, 28, 29, 30, back cover (gadget cozy)
Jason Franson/Sun Media Corporation: 45
Nigel Dobson: 46
Courtesy of RelightNY: 47
panimages inc.: 69, 70, 71, back cover (bike helmet)
Debbie Yea: 92 (Craig Battle), 93 (Susan Sinclair, Mandy Ng, Melissa Owens)
Kathy Ko: 93 (Debbie Yea)

Thanks...

To the OWL Think Tank for their ideas on pages 42—43.

If you liked
TRY this at HOME,
you'll love OWL magazine
...the award-winning magazine created especially for kids (ages 9 to 13)

Ten times a year, *OWL* subscribers get a fun package of do-it-yourself activities, comics, puzzles and articles on current issues – all designed to help them actively explore and think about their world and prepare for their teen years.

OWL Magazine...a must-read for preteens!

Subscribe today at
www.owlkids.com/trythis
or call 1-800-551-6957

ENVIRONMENTAL BENEFITS STATEMENT

Owlkids saved the following resources by printing the pages of this book on chlorine free paper made with 10% post-consumer waste.

TREES	WATER	ENERGY	SOLID WASTE	GREENHOUSE GASES
4	1,333	3	221	407
FULLY GROWN	GALLONS	MILLION BTUs	POUNDS	POUNDS

Calculations based on research by Environmental Defense and the Paper Task Force. Manufactured at Friesens Corporation

Celebrate Earth Day on April 22!